A Story By Book

Copyright 2019 Pauline Roberts
All rights reserved.

No part of this publication may be reproduced or transmitted in any form or by any means, electronic or mechanical, including photocopy, recording or any information storage and retrieval system now known or to be invented, without permission in writing from the author.

ISBN: 9781645503750
Library of Congress Cataloging in Publication Data

Daddy reads to Baby
A Story By Book

By
Pauline Roberts
Illustrated by Keith Conner

Suddenly, Baby grabs me.

"Baby loves me," I smile.

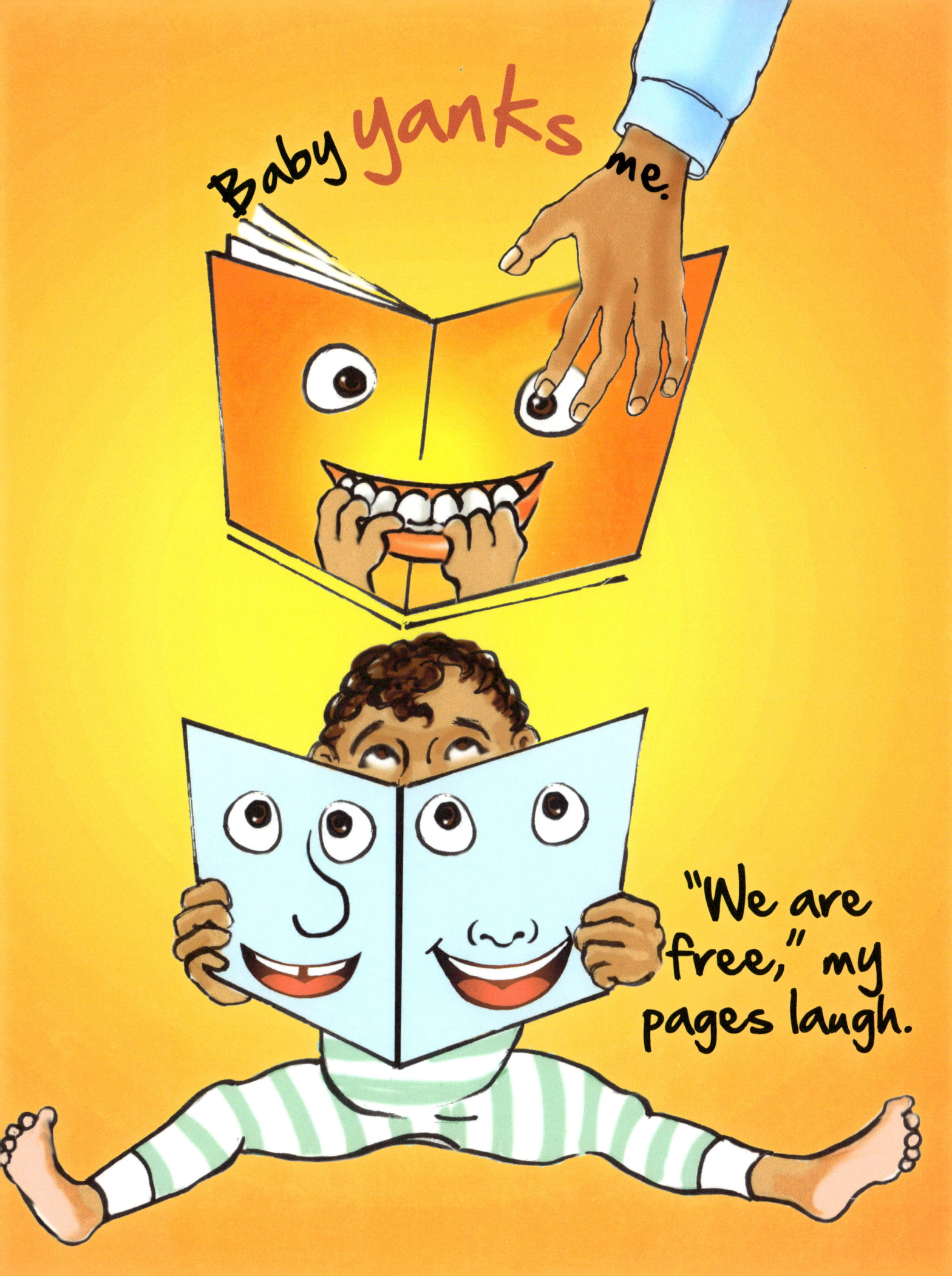

I am *glad*.

She opens my covers and my pages fall. I hear Catherine *gasp!*

It's nippy! I shiver.

I think Baby likes my story.

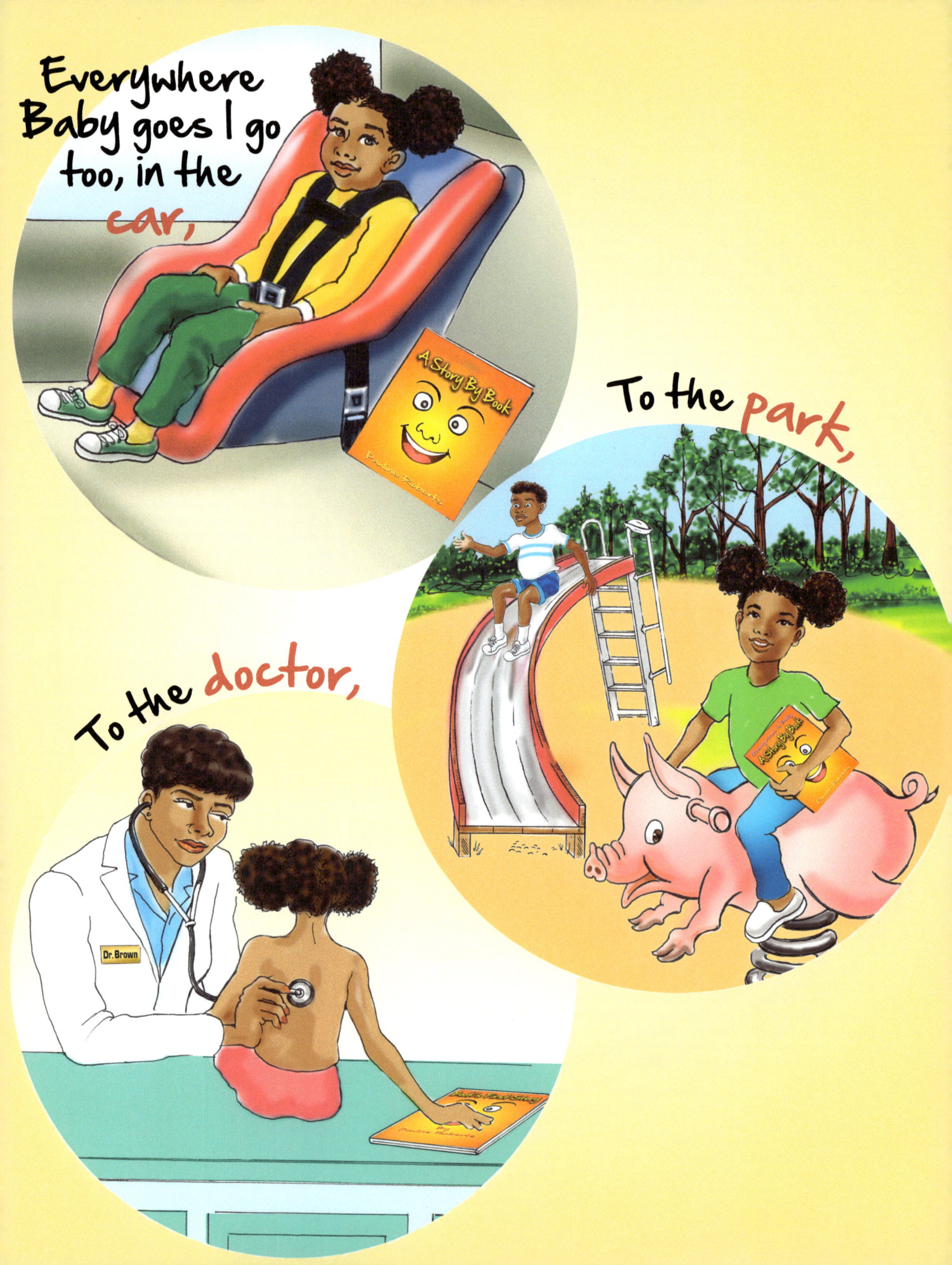

And to **bed**. Baby is my best friend, and I am Baby's **favorite storybook!**

The end.

www.ingramcontent.com/pod-product-compliance
Lightning Source LLC
Chambersburg PA
CBHW041120070526
44584CB00002B/222